Machines That Work

Big Tractors

Amy Hayes

Cavendish
Square

New York

Published in 2016 by Cavendish Square Publishing, LLC
243 5th Avenue, Suite 136, New York, NY 10016

Copyright © 2016 by Cavendish Square Publishing, LLC

First Edition

Library of Congress Cataloging-in-Publication Data

Hayes, Amy.
Big tractors / Amy Hayes.
pages cm. — (Machines that work)
Includes index.
ISBN 978-1-50260-401-9 (hardcover) ISBN 978-1-50260-400-2 (paperback) ISBN 978-1-50260-402-6 (ebook)
1. Farm tractors—Juvenile literature. 2. Tillage—Juvenile literature. I. Title.

S711.H39 2016
631.3—dc23

2015006123

Editorial Director: David McNamara
Copy Editor: Rebecca Rohan
Art Director: Jeff Talbot
Designer: Stephanie Flecha
Senior Production Manager: Jennifer Ryder-Talbot
Production Editor: Renni Johnson
Photo Research: J8 Media

The photographs in this book are used by permission and through the courtesy of: Mike Powles/Photolibrary/Getty Images, cover; Boomer Jerritt/All Canada Photos/Getty Images, 5; SimplyCreativePhotography/E+/Getty Images, 7; Vstock LLC/Getty Images, 9; Henry Arden/Cultura/Getty Images, 11; Bloomberg/Getty Images, 13; brytta/E+/Getty Images, 15; Juan Silva/The Image Bank/Getty Images, 17; David Reede/All Canada Photos/Getty Images, 19; Photo Researchers/Science Source/Getty Images, 21.

Printed in the United States of America

Contents

Tractors are hard workers!

4

Tractors are found on farms.

Tractors have big **engines**.

9

The engines help them
pull **implements**.

11

Tractors pull **hay balers**.

13

Tractors pull **spreaders**.

14

They help **prepare** the fields for new plants to grow.

They help harvest food.

18

19

Tractors work hard in the fields.

New Words

engine (EN-jin) A machine that changes energy into motion.

hay balers (HAY BAYL-erz) Machines that take hay and form it into blocks.

implements (IM-ple-mentz) An object that does work.

prepare (pre-PAIR) To get ready for.

spreaders (SPRED-derz) Machines that pull new dirt across a field.

Index

23

About the Author

Amy Hayes lives in the beautiful city of Buffalo, New York. She has written several books for children, including the Machines That Work and the Our Holidays series for Cavendish Square.

About BOOK WORMS

Bookworms help independent readers gain reading confidence through high-frequency words, simple sentences, and strong picture/text support. Each book explores a concept that helps children relate what they read to the world in which they live.